Today I Am a Ma'am

Today I Am a Ma'am

*and Other Musings on Life,
Beauty, and Growing Older*

VALERIE HARPER

WITH CATHERINE WHITNEY

Illustrations by Rick Tulka

Cliff Street Books

An Imprint of HarperCollins*Publishers*

HarperCollins books may be purchased for educational, business, or sales promotional use. For information please write: Special Markets Department, HarperCollins Publishers Inc., 10 East 53rd Street, New York, NY 10022.

FIRST EDITION

Designed by William Ruoto

Library of Congress Cataloging-in-Publication Data

Harper, Valerie, 1940–
      Today I Am a Ma'am : and other musings on life, beauty, and growing older / Valerie Harper with Catherine Whitney.
          p.   cm.
        ISBN 0-06-019929-6
        1. Women—Humor.   2. Middle-aged women—Humor.   I. Whitney, Catherine.   II. Title.

PN6231.W6 H35 2001
305.4'02'07—dc21   00-065911

01 02 03 04 05 ❖/QW 10 9 8 7 6 5 4 3 2 1

To my darlings,
Tony and Cristina,
and for women of a certain age
everywhere

Contents

Contents

Contents

Contents

Acknowledgments

I hope you have as much fun reading this book as I had writing it. I want to thank my coauthor, Catherine Whitney, for her wonderful work, her invaluable guidance, and for all the laughter we shared. She not only took my words and crafted them beautifully but she also further enhanced the book by bringing two people of enormous humor and creativity into the project—her writing partner, Paul Krafin, who is a very funny man, and our extremely talented illustrator, Rick Tulka.

I'm very grateful to Jane Dystel, my crackerjack literary agent, for her tenacity, keen attention to detail, and for her belief in me.

Thank you to my editor, Diane Reverand, whose creativity, enthusiasm, and savvy have infused the process from the beginning. She has been a joy to work with. Diane's associate, Janet Dery, saw the book's production through with patience and great organizational skills, and we'd have been lost without her.

I want to acknowledge the dear, beautiful, brilliant women who for decades have been my "girlfriends." Special thanks to Penny Almog, Nicole Barth, and Iva Rifkin for the insights you contributed to the book and for all you've shared over the years. I want to thank Charlotte Brown, Sue Cameron, Joanne Carson, Arlene Golonka, and Carol Kane, as well, for telling your stories and giving me so much loving support.

I treasure my relationships with each of you, and it looks like we got a book out of it.

Today I Am a Ma'am

CHAPTER 1

PARDON ME, MA'AM

Little Old Ladies

I knew I had to write this book the day I found myself uttering a shocking statement. I

was regaling my teenage daughter, Cristina, with a funny story about an encounter I'd had with a woman at the supermarket. "She was this little old lady of sixty," I said. That's as far as I got, because Cristina was doubled over with laughter.

"What?" I demanded, annoyed. "I didn't get to the punch line yet."

"Uh, Mom," she said with a grin, "I hate to break it to you, but *you're* sixty."

"So?"

"You just said, 'this little old lady of sixty.'"

"Oh, my God!" It was a moment of truth. I certainly didn't consider myself to be a little old lady, but if the phrase could slip off my tongue with such remarkable ease, that meant it was hardwired in my brain.

Shelf Life

I never thought I'd be sixty. It's not that I didn't expect to live this long. It's just that—well, sixty! That's almost old. I was afraid that by the time I reached fifty I wouldn't be *myself* anymore. I guess that when you spend your life as a dancer and an actor you learn to view the passing of time like the ticking of a time bomb—*five more years until annihilation . . . four more years until annihilation . . . thirty minutes until annihilation.* I can still remember being a thirteen-year-old ballet dancer and thinking, oh, my God, if I don't get into a ballet company by age sixteen, I'm sunk. Imagine feeling that pressure at thirteen!

That's an extreme example, but the prevailing media wisdom is that women have shelf life. If you don't believe it, just look at the movies. When was the last time you saw a leading man of a certain age (Sean Connery, Michael Douglas) paired with a leading lady (Meryl Streep, Faye Dunaway) of a similar certain age? What does it say about our society when our most popular romantic male leads are in their fifties, sixties, and even seventies, and our most popular female romantic leads

Woman as packaged goods.

are in their twenties and thirties? If I were to be cast in a Harrison Ford movie, I'd probably get the role of his mother. I'm not joking. Jane Fonda once made this observation: "What's the worst thing about being a female movie star over forty? Watching each year as Robert Redford's leading ladies get younger and younger."

What a Greeting

For pure, unadulterated insults, nothing beats a trip down the greeting card aisle. Those warm, fuzzy greeting card moments are certainly not directed at women—especially past the age of thirty. I ask you, who writes these cards? A troll in the back room? Here's a random selection. You be the judge.

Birthdays are like fine wine.
Once you find an age you like, stick to it!

Birthdays mean nothing to women like us.

Why, you and I are just a couple of teenagers stuck in middle-aged bodies . . .

And deep, deep denial.

Birthdays are like French fries.

The more we have, the bigger our butts get.

A birthday and big boobs.

Well, at least you've got one of those things today.

Happy Birthday, Gal!

No need to panic yet . . .

Your whole butt still fits in the mirror.

To aid you on your birthday, here are some valuable lovemaking tips for people your age . . .

Set alarm clock for 2 minutes in case you doze off in the middle.

Make sure you put 911 on speed dial.

Trapped in the greeting card aisle.

Keep extra Polygrip close by so your teeth don't end up under the bed.

Have heating pads, Tylenol, splints, and crutches ready in case you actually complete the act.

We know we're getting older when "Frosted Flakes" begins to refer to our peer group.

Here's the real kicker. You don't have to be over forty to be pronounced over the hill. I saw this card for a woman turning thirty:

Wow, 30! You know what *that* means!

Time to get a bad haircut and some real dowdy clothes.

If Life Imitated Television . . .

Teenagers would be twenty-five, Mom would be thirty, and Grandma would be thirty-three. Are there any real people left?

Two years ago, I shot an NBC television pilot for a wonderful show called *Thicker Than Water.* The plot centered around a family in New Jersey. Ron Leibman and I played a blue-collar couple whose two adult offspring were suddenly returning to the nest. The script was funny and real, and we had a great response from the studio audience. Our hopes were high.

NBC tested the pilot. The marketing guy came back to us with the results. "It tested great in the demographic between ages eighteen and forty-nine," he reported.

I was thrilled. "Wonderful!"

He held up a cautionary finger. "The problem is, it tested poorly in the thirteen to eighteen demographic."

I didn't get it. "Why is that a problem?"

He gave me a pitying look. "We can't sell a program to advertisers without that demographic."

Oh. Silly me. I guess I missed the memo that explained how fifteen-year-olds were the

Gold Standard for all television viewing. Maybe *Thicker Than Water* would have had a better chance if the twenty-something kids had an actress of thirty playing Mom.

Ageism is practiced by the networks, because that's what Madison Avenue dictates. But how do they explain away the decline in viewership? How does it make sense to say, "You're over fifty. We don't care what you watch?" Imagine a supermarket chain deciding they're only going to count groceries sold to people under thirty. Youth obsession is killing us.

And yet . . . you and I know that we grown-up women are a powerful force. The youth-addled brains in Hollywood just don't get it. It's time for a call to arms, and I'm leading the charge. I figured I was the right one for the job, because women of a certain age often come up to me in restaurants and on the street and just start chatting, as if we were picking up a conversation that had been going on for a long time. There's a comfort level there, an ability to be perfectly frank.

One woman told me, "When Rhoda and Mary talked about turning thirty in an epidode titled 'Today I Am a Ma'am,' it was extremely comforting." It's something I've heard a lot. *The Mary Tyler Moore Show* was the first to feature women who were not only single and thirty but also on their own and enjoying themselves. Now it's time to break another mold—to say, "Today I really *am* a ma'am!"

My goal is to give women a laugh, a bit of encouragement, a brighter view of themselves. Behind every joke is a truth. When we laugh at ourselves, we're happier. When we poke fun at the bizarre standards by which we are judged, we gain confidence.

It's Our Turn

It feels good to talk back to the outrageous youth obsession that afflicts our culture. I can't stand how grim everyone is about aging, as if it were a shameful secret. Osteoporosis, liver spots, vaginal dryness—oh, please! But I hate the other side of it, too. All those phony "fabulous at fifty" books written by people who never met a cellulite pocket. Face it. We aren't all jumping for joy at being older. You don't hear women waxing poetic about their alligator skin or the way their breasts are heading south. The point is, we can still be great. We can still be happy. And we can figure out, with humor, what it means to be us at this age.

I'm enjoying this stage of my life. It doesn't take me as much time to get going anymore. There was a point, not that long ago, when I wouldn't leave the house without full makeup. Now you're lucky if I bother to apply the line eraser makeup to the circles under my eyes.

There have been other surprising benefits. I've discovered the joy of crankiness. I no longer feel compelled to be such a pleaser. And, while no one would ever accuse me of being serene, I find that it's easier for me to get over disappointments. The voice of experience speaks to me, reminding me that nothing is ever life or death—except, of course, life and death. What a wonderful freedom there is as we grow older.

I'm here to tell you that now it's my turn—or I should say, *our* turn. Women live with a giant boulder hanging over our heads called fat, or old, or ugly. We're always staring up at it, worrying that it's going to come crashing down to crush us. Enough already.

CHAPTER 2

DE'MEAN STREETS

Just Chicks

To be a woman of any age in America today is to take a walk down *de'mean* streets.

We've come a long way, baby—but why are you still calling us baby?

- Why are blondes dumb and ditzy?
- What is the male equivalent of *bimbo?*

There are countless ways women are discounted. It matters what you call something.

I think I understand why women loved Rhoda so much. It was because she refused to be demeaned. She wasn't the typical American sweetheart—not the soft, compliant, blue-eyed blonde. Rhoda wasn't a prom queen. She was a real woman. She cracked jokes to cover her fears and insecurities. She worried about her weight. She was just like you and me. She walked de'mean streets with a swagger.

Even so, when I look back thirty years, I find myself somewhat amazed by the self-deprecating tone that was part of Rhoda's signature. There's an underlying mix of guilt and inadequacy that belies Rhoda's power.

For me, the great fun of playing Rhoda was her mixture of insecurity and great bravado. Remember the lines she spoke at the beginning of each episode?

My name is Rhoda Morgenstern.

I was born in the Bronx, New York, in December 1941.

I've always felt responsible for World War II.

The first thing I remember liking that liked me back was food.

I had a bad puberty; it lasted seventeen years.

I'm a high school graduate. I went to art school. My entrance exam was on a book of matches.

I decided to move out of the house when I was twenty-four. My mother still refers to this as the time I ran away from home.

Eventually I ran to Minneapolis, where it's cold and I figured I'd keep better.

Now I'm back in Manhattan. New York—this is your last chance!

The writers consistently wrote Rhoda and the other characters as hilarious but authentic human beings. Viewers identified with them. As my dear pal Nicole once observed, "Mary is who you want to be. Rhoda is who you probably are. And Phyllis is who you're afraid you'll become."

Smoke and Mirrors

I have never met a woman, no matter how beautiful or self-confident, who could face a mirror without cringing. Especially when that mirror wages a sneak attack. You're running to catch a bus and catch a side view of your sagging jawline in a store window. Or you're all dressed up for a party and your friendly bathroom mirror is telling you that you look fabulous. Then, in the course of the evening, you enter a restaurant ladies' room with lights so bright you think you're in a police lineup, and you can see every flaw and bulge.

Reality check. When you look in the mirror, what do you see? Sometimes I think that women's mirrors have been fitted with those special fun house warp features. Or maybe it's all mirrors. My friend Sue, a real liver of life and a recent enrollee in tap classes, describes standing within a group of dance students and catching a glimpse of a sadly sagging pair of knees in the mirror. "God, whose knees are those?" she thought with pity. Her eyes slid up the body until she was staring into her own face. "Oh, no!" she yelled, horrified, stopping the class in its tracks.

A perfectly attractive woman can stand in front of a mirror and see the Pillsbury Doughgirl.

The Friendly Skies

Recently, a male acquaintance who travels a lot for business was complaining about

"I can't go out looking like this!"

TULKA

what he perceived to be the deterioration of the flight attendant—or, as he said, the "stewardess." He reminisced longingly about the good old days when flying the friendly skies meant being served by young beauties with perfect bodies, dazzling smiles, and doormat demeanors. Today's flight attendants are male and female, old and young, multi-ethnic, and efficient without being slavish. They're working men and women, not club hostesses.

Flight attendants today look like America. In the 1940s, an aspiring flight attendant had to be single, female, white, under age twenty-seven, between 105 and 125 pounds, and between 5 feet 2 inches and 5 feet 7 inches. She could have no physical abnormalities, including wearing glasses.

Who were these girls? Beauty pageant runners-up? Former fashion models? The American ideal? More likely, the ideal of male airline executives and their marketing consultants.

Men, like my acquaintance who misses flying the good old skies when women were girls, should ask themselves whether they'd rather have a dewy-eyed, compliant girl or a strong, authoritative, well-trained woman around in case of an emergency.

Got Milk?

It's impossible to talk about women and food service without talking about breasts. Breasts are getting bigger and higher, and it's not because women are more comfortable or look more "natural" carrying around over-stuffed mammaries. They're doing it for the consumer—and I don't mean infants. The new look in breasts is a gravity-defying feat. High and firm like a presentational display. Like a platter being offered: "Coffee, tea, or milk?"

Breasts that say, "We're here to serve you."

Edibles: Women as Snack Food

Here's some food for thought. Have you ever noticed how often women get referred to as edibles? Usually they're described as a dessert and are almost always sweet, spicy, or juicy. Consider:

Cookie
Sugar
Honey
Hot tamale
Cupcake
Tomato

Most women would have no trouble using any of these delectables in a sentence. We've heard them all.

"Sweetie pie, you look good enough to eat."

"Hey, baby cakes!"

"Honey bun, give me a little sugar."

My new favorite is "arm candy"—a

term used to describe a beautiful woman on the arm of a powerful man. Ask yourself: Do you want to be with a man who thinks of you as a Snickers bar?

Oh, Grow Up!

It's not sour grapes when I say that our culture has been trampled by the supremacy of youth. Hard bodies and unformed minds. I can still remember a time when one's value was defined by experience and ability. We all longed for those precious credits and were proud when we could add them to our résumés. Not anymore.

A dear friend of mine, who also happens to be one of the great creative geniuses of our business, told me about applying to work on the creation of a show. The woman who interviewed him was twenty-two, and he immediately saw that his name didn't ring a bell. So he

"Sugar and spice and everything nice."

TULKA

started to name some of the hit shows he'd worked on in the seventies and eighties. The girl's face registered a glimmer of recognition, followed by a look that is generally reserved for sniffing old meat. "Yeah, I've seen them on late-night cable," she said, dismissing him to the rest home.

You'd think writers would be less affected by ageism than actors, but not so. I know older writers working today in Hollywood who hire young people to pose as their "partners" in business meetings to make them seem more hip.

I say, let's not sit here and take it anymore. After all, we're the majority; we can influence the types of movies and TV shows out there.

What do you suppose would happen if one million women, between the ages of forty and sixty-five, petitioned producers and commercial sponsors for more quality programming featuring women their age? Maybe it would wake them up.

Years ago, Mary Tyler Moore said to

me, "Val, did you ever walk into a restaurant and wonder if they're looking at you because you're beautiful, or they're looking at you because you're famous? Does that ever bother you?"

I laughed. "No, I've never lost sleep worrying that people only looked at me for my beauty." I got her point, though. Deep down, every woman wants to be loved and admired for who she is on the inside, but we all know that the world judges us first from the outside.

CHAPTER 3

TULKA

TYRANNIES OLD AND NEW

Barbie's War Chest

Barbie ran for president in the year 2000. You may have heard about her campaign.

Although she never made it onto the electoral map, a campaign by America's perfect doll is interesting to contemplate: What exactly propelled Barbie to enter the race? It's not as if she didn't have a very satisfying career—or twelve—already. Astronaut, doctor, airline pilot, princess, Olympian, career woman, cabana girl. Where did she ever find the time?

If you ask me, the motivation was clothes. Just think about the wardrobe involved in running for president!

She's got her tailored suits with skirts, her tailored suits with pants, modest heels, Habitat for Humanity workshirts and boots, straw hats, baseball caps, campaign T-shirts, picnic attire, jogging outfits, winter wool (not fur) for the chilly North, a smashing fundraiser wardrobe—the list is endless. Then, of course, if she wins, there's the Inaugural gown and Ken's stylish tux.

Sometimes it seems as if everything in life comes down to clothes.

Sizing Down

I've been hitting the shopping racks for many moons. I'm old enough to remember when the odd-numbered sizes were introduced. Now we had a choice—not just sizes eight, ten, and twelve but also sizes seven, nine, and eleven. My mom used to insist that the odd numbers were better for us "short-waisted" girls. I knew being short-waisted was a hideous affliction, because she always looked sympathetic when she said it. You don't hear much about short-waistedness these days.

At some point in the seventies, I began to notice an interesting ruse being perpetrated by the fashion industry. A size eight was no longer a true eight. It was really a ten or a twelve. Maybe this is where the term "downsizing" came from. Oh, we women knew the scam. We weren't fooled. But we gladly participated in it. "Look, honey, I'm still a size ten."

When I was filming *Rhoda*, I was always on or falling off a diet, so setting wardrobe was a challenge. Our wardrobe supervisor would hold up various items and ask, "Are you going to attempt to get into these today?" I had "attempt pants" and I also had a couple of "attempt suits." Some of my attempt clothes have yet to be worn to this day. I'm still attempting, but not so hard anymore.

Being and Nothingness

When I was in grade school, shopping with Mom became a deeply humiliating experience. She would take me by the hand, march me up to the saleslady, and, turning up the volume on her voice, ask, "Miss, where can I find the *chubby* sizes?" The Chubby Department became the bane of my early existence and I resented that the male equivalent was called *husky*. Husky seemed a more favorable image—a powerful arctic dog as opposed to a fat kid.

I was conditioned early on to be size conscious—thus eight was perfect, ten was acceptable, twelve was heading toward chubby. The standards have undergone a dramatic shift, like everything else in our society. Perfection is shrinking.

My daughter and I were out shopping recently when I discovered a rack of hip, fashionable clothes. They were size zero. At first I thought my eyes were playing tricks. They must have been size ten. But no, on closer inspection, the clothes were size zero.

What a strange race of alien creatures these must be, those who wear no size of clothing. Not size one or two. Even infinitesimal-seeming size four is a beached whale next to a size zero.

Zero represents a state of nil. Neither above nor below. Not minus one or plus one. The place of nothing that is between the two. An empty space. My big toe wouldn't fit through the leg of a pair of size zero pants. My right breast couldn't manage to contain itself in a size zero top.

Talk about raising the bar while lowering the standards of reality: Isn't all fashion a conspiracy to force us constantly to redefine our image of ourselves and what is deemed culturally acceptable? And by doing so, to sell us the fabulous new fall fashion line? It's commerce. Not sociology, not psychology. Cloth. Goods. Money.

Women are highly susceptible to the siren call of fashion. Otherwise, why were we walking around in cropped pants that ended somewhere between our calves and our ankles last summer? Who decided that would be a good idea? So attractive. Someone, somewhere, is having an awfully good laugh on all of the rest of us. They're probably wearing those cropped pants, too. Handmade. That's the look. It's theirs. They said it would be so, and we (the fashion-conscious public) lined up for our cropped pants.

But size zero cropped pants! What waif-like figure inhabits that airy realm? What fluke of genetics or life of starvation leads to size zero? If you are no size, what size actually is it that you are wearing? Does it take less cloth to make something of no size than it does to make the same piece as a size one? How much of something without a size can one person turn out in a day?

My daughter tells me that it's a ludicrous but real status symbol in her generation of younger women to wear a size zero. I tremble at the future possibilities. Size double zero. Size triple zero. Size minus fifteen. Where are we going? What if you have a body? Like a woman? Are we headed for a time when we'll be embarrassed to say, "I'm a size two"?

Witches' Brew

Most women seem to accept the fact that you have to suffer for beauty. There's no better example of that than the act of applying hot wax to the most sensitive areas of our

The incredible shrinking garment.

bodies in order to render them hairless. I still remember the day Iva and I discovered the Hot Wax Torture Chamber.

We were young Broadway dancers at the time. We held one dancer named Nancy in especially high esteem. She was absolutely gorgeous, and her legs were long and as smooth as silk. Nancy's secret was her own special waxing brew. She agreed to give us a lesson.

With hope and some trepidation, Iva and I entered Nancy's dressing room to find a pot of wax simmering on a hot plate. We watched with a mixture of horror and fascination as Nancy carefully spread the melted green wax on her legs with a kitchen spatula. Then she laid strips of wax paper on top of the wax, making sort of a leg sandwich. She smiled at us placidly. "Now we wait a moment."

I knew what was coming next. "I can't watch," I groaned.

Nancy laughed. "Oh, it doesn't hurt at all," she lied. Without flinching, she pulled the wax paper off her legs in strips and showed us the accursed hairs captured in the effort.

"Your turn," she announced cheerfully.

Well, pain is relative. If you were to compare Nancy's wax treatment to, say, having a root canal without Novocain, waxing was a breeze. Compared to falling off a cliff and smashing your head against sharp rocks, waxing was a walk in the park. But painless it was not. Iva and I staggered out of Nancy's dressing room, our beet-red legs smarting as if we'd just applied a blowtorch. Thank God it wasn't a matinee day.

That wasn't the end of it, though. Even with the pain, the result seemed worth it. So Iva and I invested in our own supplies. A few weeks later, we gave ourselves a good waxing at home. Left unsupervised, we were a disaster. I guess we left it on too long, and the wax hardened into a bricklike mass and wouldn't come off. We spent hours chipping at the wax with emery boards, but we still had the vestiges of green wax bits on our legs a week later. I joked that maybe we could donate our legs to Madam Tussaud's Wax Museum.

Nancy's Hot Wax Treatment.
It was a true witches' brew.

TULKA

Bad Hair Days

To be accurate, it's not really bad hair *days*. It's bad hair *years*. Bad hair *decades*. Bad hair *eras*. As a member of the naturally frizzy hair club, I have spent my life seeking a reprieve from nature. When I was a girl, my mother used to tell me, "You're so lucky to have naturally curly hair." That was fine during the pin-curl fifties, but then the straight-haired sixties hit and my luck ran out. I tried everything imaginable to achieve the sleek look of the times. I slathered my locks with a green or lavender glop called Wave Set that plastered them to my head with the force of epoxy. I used rollers the size of coffee cans. In desperation, I once tried ironing my hair and practically set fire to my head.

As hairstyles changed, I gamely tried to keep pace. I teased and sprayed and blow-dried and even chemically straightened. Then, noticing the white hairs nestled in the curls, I started coloring. Endless hours pursuing beauty! As Lily Tomlin once asked, "If truth is beauty, how come no one has their hair done in a library?"

Female Bondage

Last year I guest-starred in an episode of *Sex and the City,* the sizzling HBO series. Well, forget the sex. Let's talk about the shoes! It was like joining the Mile High Club!

Every year, the heels get higher and the podiatrists get richer. We abhor the hideous practice of foot binding but see nothing wrong with accepting a fashion mandate that is crippling.

After decades of stumbling through life on spikes, platforms, stilettos, toe-crushing pointy pumps, cutting strappy sandals, and backless mules, I have been liberated in midlife from the need to wobble. I have given up footwear by the Inquisition. Frankly, I just don't care anymore if my calves look shapely. These days, comfort trumps style.

It's tough to go straight.

"Somebody get me down from here!"

TULKA

Then and Now

THEN

In the fifties and sixties we wore sleeveless dresses with impunity. It never occurred to us to do upper arm upkeep. Our arms were our arms—hefty or thin, muscular or wobbly. If you don't believe me, check out the family photo album. I'll bet you'll find pictures of Mom, Grandma, and Great-Grandma sitting around the picnic table sans sleeves.

NOW

Sleevelessness has made a major comeback, just in time for my midlife jiggle. But today's unsleeved arms are toothpick thin and hard as steel. They don't have any of that good old-fashioned "Sorry, I knocked the lemonade pitcher off the table" swing.

THEN

The full-figured woman—as represented by Jane Russell and Marilyn Monroe. These weren't skinny little girls with blowup breasts. Their tops and bottoms actually matched. And God forbid you should see a ripple of muscle on a 1950s beauty. In *Annie Get Your Gun*, the Frank Butler song went "The girl that I marry will have to be as soft and as pink as a nursery."

Lady Marlene leveled the playing field for us less-than-endowed dancers of the fifties. The Lady Marlene Push-up Bra was foam rubber covered in nylon fabric. Your breasts spilled out of the top.

NOW

As a ballet dancer in the "soft" fifties, I was very self-conscious about my calves of steel. You'd think I'd be delighted to welcome the era of strong, fit, muscled women. While I'm a great proponent of physical power for women, today's version brings a whole new tyranny: "Show your muscles, girls (through your God-given fat layer), and let's see some cleavage, too." Let's face it. Working, sweating, pounding off the adipose

Do you remember when women wore bathing caps with large hoop earrings attached? The point couldn't have been to look attractive. Maybe the hoops were supposed to double as emergency life preservers. Maybe they were intended for poolside fortune telling.

tissue while maintaining or developing breasts is a major hat trick.

THEN

You wouldn't be caught dead with bra straps showing. (I used to pin them to my dress or blouse.)

NOW

The more underwear showing, the better. The bra as outerwear.

THEN

Full encasement in industrial-strength girdles.

NOW

Thongs. (To quote the actress Minnie Driver, "Me bum has eaten me knickers.")

THEN

Gloves. As my mother instructed, "A lady never goes out without her gloves."

NOW

Gloves are used only for weddings, ski trips, and home burglaries.

THEN

Ladies' dresses, suits, stockings with seams, garter belts, hats.

NOW

Miniskirts, tank tops, sneakers, jeans, flip-flops, work boots, ten-inch heels.

CHAPTER 4

JUST DESSERTS

———

Let Us Eat Cake

I can remember that cake box like it was yesterday. The bright red Dugan's logo. The dried frosting stuck to the cardboard sides. Dugan's was a bakery in New Jersey that delivered pastry and cakes to our house. I was thirteen, and I was standing in the kitchen gorging myself on cake before going to dance class. I cut a slice and ate it with a glass of milk, and then another, and another. I felt a twinge because I should have been eating a healthy breakfast. Mom always cooked so sensibly—meat, potatoes, vegetables, five little lamb chops for five people. Before I knew what was happening, I had eaten another slice, and then another. I was full, but I kept on eating. I left a tiny piece so I could say I didn't eat the whole cake. I remember thinking, oh, I'll go burn this off in ballet class.

Dancing off five thousand calories! That was the beginning of my mental illness about food. It took the form of phantasmagoric self-delusion.

Favorite Diet Fibs

- It doesn't count if you eat standing up.
- There are no calories in the food you taste while cooking.
- The acid in diet soda destroys the calories in pizza.
- Taking a taste of your dining companion's food is calorie free.
- Energy bars—especially the chocolate chip coconut—make you thin.

These fibs do support your habit, but they're very funny. I went out to dinner recently with my close friend Charlotte, another bulge battler. We agreed that we were going to be "good" and really watch what we eat. But when the waiter came around, Charlotte happily reached for the bread basket. Noticing my raised eyebrows, she leaned across the table and whispered, "It's okay. I'm eating this under an assumed name."

Incognito at the dessert cart.

TULKA

The Pounder in the Valley

When I was a young actress living in California, I tried every wild scheme making the rounds to get rid of my bubble wrap thighs. My friend Iva and I used to go see a woman affectionately known as "the Pounder in the Valley." She was the size of a sumo wrestler. She and her daughter had thick, meaty hands—huge hands. They'd stretch you out on a table, face down and naked, and then literally pound the fat off your body. The Pounder was the rage then. All the big movie stars went to her. It was so painful that she would give you a towel to scream into so the neighbors wouldn't call the police. I can still remember us hobbling out, black and blue from the waist down.

Finally, Iva said to me, "I can't believe I'm paying so much money to look like I've been in a car wreck. These bruises can't be good." I agreed but moved on to the next fad—wrapping. It was guaranteed to take off inches instantly. I'd be tightly wrapped in cloth strips that had been soaked in a strange-smelling solution. I'd lie there for an hour until every drop of water was squeezed out. Voilà! Ten pounds gone—until I raced to the water fountain to rehydrate. The pounds and inches returned instantly. It was the dumbest weight loss concept ever invented.

But you see my point. Women will do anything to lose weight. Looking back, I have to laugh at some of the outrageous diets we tried. The craziest diets were those that involved eating only one or two foods for weeks on end. There was the strawberries and champagne diet, the grapefruit diet, the hard-boiled egg diet, the ice cream diet. Even ice cream can start to look sickening when it's your main staple. I recall one diet guaranteed to take off five pounds in two days. It included steak, hard-boiled eggs, lettuce leaves, and six prunes. None of these diets ever worked for long.

Here's the irony of the thin-is-in mentality, which is still pervasive: One hundred years ago, the ideal body for a woman was curvaceous. Women wanted to have meat on their bones. Lillian Russell, the turn-of-the-century femme fatale, weighed 210 pounds. Best-selling diet books had titles such as *How to Be Plump.* At that time, having meat on your bones was considered healthy.

Those were the days!

The Sliding Scale

After agonizing about my weight most of my life, I wasn't exactly thrilled to hear the news about midlife spread. Our bodies are saying, "I'm going to add a little bit of padding around your waist and hips to keep you warm in winter." And even though we say, "Don't worry. I've got a good winter coat," our bodies don't pay attention.

Take thigh bumps. To what purpose thigh bumps? Neither hip nor butt, this extra padding is located on the side of each thigh, like a protective shield. It's like having shoulder pads on your thighs, designed to save you if you're suddenly thrown against a wall. Our bodies are always trying to save us, but we don't want to be saved. When all else fails, thank God there are cover-ups.

I'm an expert at hiding fat. At some point in my life, I faced the awful truth that my hips weren't going anywhere, so my only hope was artifice. In the 1970s, I chose empire dresses with scooped necks, which either hid a multitude of sins or made me look like Valerie-the-hot-air-balloon, depending on which way the wind was blowing. With time and practice, I became a master illusionist.

I was also a proponent of corrective underwear. During our Broadway dancer days, Iva and I favored the "tube of steel" girdle. This was a girdle so tight you needed an extra twenty minutes and a can of baby powder to get it on, and then it was a challenge to walk. It literally sealed your thighs together.

No pain, no gain?

"If we're attacked we won't be able to run," I said to Iva as we headed out one evening.

"So what if he catches us," she laughed. "He'll never get this girdle off."

Food Buddies

When I was a young dancer, one of my best friends was Gene Varrone. I met Gene in 1959 when we were in the chorus of the Broadway musical comedy *Take Me Along,* starring Jackie Gleason. Gene and I were pals, confidants, and food buddies. On matinee days, we'd sneak off together to the Acropolis Diner on Eighth Avenue in New York City. They had wonderful lemon soup with rice, moussaka, baklava—the works. The waiters were tall and swarthy, and Gene claimed they were all in love with me, but I think they just saw two compulsive eaters walking in and said, "Hey, big check coming." Elderly Greek men in fedoras and short-sleeved shirts would sit around playing cards in the corner and drinking ouzo while Gene and I shared enormous portions and the stories of our lives.

I'll never forget once Gene told me about a conversation he'd had with his psychiatrist about his weight problem. He'd been in therapy for four years, and he finally asked the doctor, "Do you think I'm really sick?" "No," she said, "you just like to eat."

Sometimes Gene and I would go on diets together, but we were both such cheaters. We'd be out to lunch, and we'd tell the waitress emphatically, "No fries, please." Then the plates showed up piled with fries.

"It's God's will," I'd whisper.

Once we were on a really strict diet and were doing quite well. Gene came over for dinner one night and I served salad with no dressing and dried apricots for dessert.

At three o'clock in the morning I called Gene. "Look, I'm cooking spaghetti. You want to come over?" He jumped in a cab.

So, what's the shame about eating? There's a line in Henry Jaglom's wonderful film, *Eating:* "Food is to women today what sex was in the fifties."

Forbidden pleasure. How many women are secret eaters?

Somebody Call the Cops

In 1967 when my first husband, Dick, was filming *The Russians Are Coming! The Russians Are Coming!* I got to know Jonathan Winters. I'll never forget being out to dinner with Jonathan when he started to argue with himself about ordering dessert: "No, no, you won't have that cake, you're fat as a pig—*I'll eat what I want*—Listen, I've had about enough of you—*Shut up, I'm ordering*—Fatty, fatty, two by four—*I'll eat cake and I'll eat it with ice cream!*"

My friend Carol, who had always been

thin as a rail, was complaining about how she couldn't stop eating. "I used to have a voice in my head that would tell me, 'No, don't take that. Don't have that. Stop.' I don't have a voice anymore. I just eat until there's no more food." Boy, I know how that feels. I was the queen of the crash diet. Up and down, yo-yo style. There's a food fool in a lot of women. Wouldn't it be great to get rid of it!

Busted

Speaking of cops . . .

Some women feel a certain embarrassment about admitting that we're on a diet. For some reason we think thin thighs are worth more if they're endowed naturally. Although I have a long history of sneaking "goodies," I have occasionally extended my sneaking to diet foods. One day I was driving in Beverly Hills, drinking a can of

"Put the chips down and come out with your hands up!"

Slim•Fast. A policeman pulled up behind me on his motorcycle. He was young and tan and handsome, and he was motioning me to pull over. I checked my face in the mirror, ran my fingers through my hair, and stuck my Slim•Fast can under the seat. When he walked up to the driver's side window, I gave him my best smile. "Yes, officer, how can I help you?"

He didn't smile back. "Show me the can, lady," he ordered, peering past me into the car.

"What can?" I asked brightly.

"You know what can. The beer can."

I just kept smiling. "Why?" I asked stupidly. For some reason, I preferred him to think I was drinking a beer than to admit I was guzzling Slim•Fast on the road.

"Come on, lady." He was getting impatient.

"Look," I offered, "I'll take the test, walk a straight line, whatever you want. Breathalyze me. You'll see I'm not drunk."

"Just-show-me-the-can."

So I reached down and pulled out the can of strawberry Slim•Fast. He gaped at it, and then he started to roar with laughter. I could still hear him long after his motorcycle had gone a half mile down the road.

Weighty Matters

Many of Rhoda's jokes focused on weight—although Rhoda was hardly fat. She just wasn't rail thin like Mary. In one episode, Rhoda ran into a guy with her car and took the opportunity to get a date. After she hit him, she asked him to dinner. Later she was at Mary's apartment all excited about her date. Mary offered her a snack—some bacon curls—and she refused, saying, "I gotta lose ten pounds before eight o'clock." That line got incredible laughs from the studio audience.

Driving under the influence of Slim•Fast.

Then Rhoda's date showed up at the door, accompanied by his cute little blond wife. Rhoda introduced him to Mary: "Mary, this is my date, Mr. and Mrs. Armand Linton." Then Rhoda proceeded to dump the bacon curls into her lap and start shoveling them into her mouth. The audience roared.

Looking back, I see that under the humor was actually a kind of sad truth. Way before I was cast in the role of Rhoda, I had the art of self-deprecation down pat from long years of practice. I didn't have great writers handing me punch lines, but I carried around my own arsenal. When I was an aspiring actress, and obsessive about my weight, my roommate Arlene once said, "You crack me up. When you walk into a room, it's as if you announce, 'Hello, I'm Valerie Harper and I'm fat. There! I said it before you did.'" She was right. And I wasn't fat, even if I wasn't Twiggy-thin, either. But think about it—at least in the days of Rhoda, they scripted a character who was worried about her weight, who talked about eating and being fat, who said things like, "I thought chocolate was a major food group." You never even see that today. I've heard casting people make remarks like "Look at her. She's fat as a pig." And this is about an actress who is perfectly normal. When I filmed a guest appearance on *Melrose Place,* I felt as if I'd been dropped onto another planet. Those kids are beautiful. Other humans pale in comparison. But they actually said, with straight faces, "Ordinary people can relate to us. We're just like them."

These were women with thighs so narrow that you could drive a truck through the space between them. And yet these young beauties were discussing ways they could trim down their already perfect legs. In the lengthy catalog of frivolous obsessions that engage women, I confess that the state of my thighs has always been front and center. I'm not especially proud of all the hours I've spent over the years bemoaning the lack of breathing room between my thighs, or the abject envy I've felt toward women who have gorgeous, slim legs.

Well, thank God that's behind me. One of the benefits of growing older is the liberation from thigh madness. They're here, they're mine, they're fine!

The Dieter's Dilemma

Many of us think of food in one of two ways. It's either legal (a lettuce leaf) or illegal (a brownie). When I look back on my own craziness I have to laugh about it.

While I was out doing errands, I passed a bakery with a delicious-looking window display. My eyes settled on a birthday cake, piled high with creamy frosting. It wasn't my birthday, but I wouldn't be denied. With great anticipation I carried the cake out to my car, where I had planned to eat it. Well, I couldn't take it home for my family to see because I was supposed to be on a strict diet. Now I faced a dilemma. Since there was no knife in the car, how would I cut this scrumptious indiscretion? I looked around and saw that the only other shop on the block was a beauty-supply store. I ran in and bought a rattail comb, the handle of which served very nicely to cut my clandestine birthday cake.

On another occasion, in the early 1970s, while religiously following the Weight Watchers diet, I was invited to a party. I brought along my preweighed Weight Watchers dinner and felt very righteous as I ignored the sumptuous buffet the hostess had provided. But midway through the evening I experienced a crashing fall from grace. On the way to the bathroom, I passed the kitchen and I was stopped short by the sight of a large platter piled high with brownies. My favorite! I stood frozen in place, staring at the brownies. We were alone. Just me and them. I quickly gobbled three, then rearranged the others so that no one would notice. A short time later, the hostess carried in the brownie platter, warning all of us, "For those of you who don't

"I feel a binge coming on!"

indulge, these brownies have marijuana in them." I covered with a weak "No thanks," but inwardly I was screaming at myself, "You fool! You fool!" I was sick as a dog for two days.

I would have refused the pot. My down-fall was the sugar. Talk about illegal consumption! I should have stuck with the lettuce leaf.

Eat Your Heart Out

I long ago came to the understanding that the problems I once had with food were not merely about food. Eating was a way of trying to fill up the emptiness, to provide comfort. It was a substitute for love. I'm not referring to the love that comes from some-one else. The love that was missing from my life was self-love. With age I've discovered a sense of worth that makes me less hungry. A piece of cake is just a piece of cake.

CHAPTER 5

THE M WORD

Wait a Minute

It gives me pause. Why is a woman's important transition called MEN-opause?

Are we pausing from men? I know, it's Latin for monthly. But since pause means a temporary stop, then shouldn't the proper term be *men-o-end?* Contrary to popular belief, menopause has a lot to recommend it. Good-bye periods and birth control. Hello entertaining hot flashes, power surges, private summers. Many women actually find menopause liberating. If it didn't get such bad press, we'd all embrace the change of life with much more gusto. Instead, there is an aura of shame that in spite of being utterly ridiculous is hard to shake. How can women feel good about themselves when the message from society is that menopause is an embarrassment? Here's an example. A few years back, a Seattle woman requested a personalized license plate reading MENOPOZ. In a letter denying her request, the Washington State Department of Licensing wrote, "MENOPOZ is offensive to good taste and dignity." I ask you. Is that any way to talk to a woman?

If Men Had Menopause . . .

- Menopause would be a celebration. Men would hold huge ceremonial rites of passage in football stadiums.
- Menopause would be a prerequisite for running a company or running the country. Men would say, "How can women understand it if they can't experience it?"
- There would be a pill for hot flashes instead of a pill for erectile dysfunction, and it would be fully covered by the insurance companies.
- Mood swings would be considered creative, not crazy.
- Every thermostat in America would be set to "cool," even in the winter. Men would control the thermostat the way they now control the TV remote.
- There would be national symposiums on bladder control.
- Billions of dollars in research money would be devoted to eliminating any discomfort.

- There would be no menopause jokes. It wouldn't be a laughing matter.
- Companies would set up personal sick days and leaves of absence to help men through the transition. Workdays would be cut short due to bouts of fatigue.
- Menopausal buddy movies would be a hit at the box office.
- It wouldn't be called menopause. It would be called *man-o-peak* or *man-o-man*.

Crazy Ladies

The three of us were having the time of our lives. We hadn't seen one another for quite a while and the gathering had the feeling of a reunion. We were the noisiest table in the place, laughing and chatting about husbands, kids, and politics. Suddenly, I was sweating into my crudité medley. "God," I whispered, pressing the pale peach linen napkin to my moist face, "I'm having a flash and it's a big one." In unison, my friends both said, "No, you're not. It really *is* hot in here."

I called the waiter over and asked him to please turn up the air conditioning. By now the three of us were fanning ourselves, gulping water, and mopping our brows with the pretty napkins.

The waiter approached apologetically. "The air conditioning is turned all the way up," he said. "In fact, we're getting complaints that it's too cold." We stared at one another for a moment, realizing that we were having a rare bonding experience—a simultaneous hot flash.

Men will pull the menopause card whenever it suits their purpose. I once heard a guy blame the Waco tragedy on a "menopausal Attorney General"—referring to Janet Reno. Oh, yeah? And what's Newt Gingrich's excuse? Maybe men do have menopause, after all.

My friend Penny described getting older this way: "When I was eighteen, I thought

Lady Macbeth was an evil old witch. When I turned fifty, I understood Lady Macbeth. Sure, she overreacted, but look how much she'd been through." I guess you could call that the wisdom of age. I've heard that when women hit forty, their brain cells start multiplying in direct proportion to the way men's brain cells start declining. Maybe that's why men say that menopausal women are crazy. It's their last mode of defense.

The New Face of Menopause

I never pictured myself as "Valerie Harper: Menopause Spokeswoman" up on a billboard in Times Square, but there you have it. And alongside me in the giant photo were Joy Behar, cohost of *The View;* Mary Wilson of the Supremes; Suzy Chaffee, former skiing champ; Dr. Mary Jane Minkin, physician and author; Karen Giblin, founder of the Red Hot

Mamas, a menopause support group; and Janet Peckinpaugh, the news anchor who won a multimillion-dollar age discrimination suit.

The purpose was to promote a new soy menopause supplement, but the effect was to say, "Hey, world, these are the faces of menopause—and we're not shrinking violets."

This new face of menopause is women who move, women who shake. It's FLASH, a senior women's hockey team in Chicago. It's Gloria Steinem getting married for the first time at age sixty-six. It's fearless women in their fifties, sixties, seventies, and beyond. It's women like Ruth Gordon, who taught me a wonderful lesson about what it means to be an older woman.

I loved Ruth Gordon. On *Rhoda* she played Carlton the doorman's mother. I also worked with her on a TV thriller called *Don't Go to Sleep*. Acting professionally since 1915, Ruth was spiffy, eccentric, and full of life. When she was almost eighty, Ruth told me, "I made a decision a long time ago that I could get old, or I could get older. That was my choice. I didn't have the choice to stay young. I decided to get older instead of getting old. Because *old* is a destination. *Older* is a process and a path." When she died, Ruth Gordon had only gotten older. She was never old. That's wisdom.

I recently saw Barbara Walters interviewing an author who had just written a book of techniques women could use to value themselves more highly. Barbara was enthusiastic. "Try one of them on me," she urged. The woman said, "Okay, we'll do one right here. First I need to know your age." There was a long beat, then Barbara leaned forward and whispered conspiratorily, "I'll tell you during the commercial." I felt badly, not for Barbara—she can take care of herself—but about the unfair age standard foisted upon women in our society. Here was *the* Barbara Walters, a celebrated, highly successful woman not admitting her age. Granted, she didn't lie, but she sure didn't feel safe saying it. Aw, to hell with it, Babs—it's none of their business anyway!

Hot Times

My friend Sue described how she had her first hot flash while attending a bris. For those who don't know, a bris is a Jewish ceremony where a guy with a set of very sharp knives trims the foreskin from a baby boy's penis—accompanied by screaming (the mother), fainting (the father), and gulping wine (the baby). After it's over, everyone eats.

At first, she thought the wave of heat was merely a reaction to the terror she felt for the infant. Maybe someone shut off the air conditioning. No, that couldn't be it. It was the middle of winter. Then it hit her. It was a hot flash! "Imagine that," she told me later. "The baby and I were both going through hormonal transitions simultaneously."

Another friend had her first hot flash in the supermarket. She was looking for an item in the freezer case. She just leaned in and closed her eyes. The cold air felt so good. She basked in the icy breeze, imagining a vacation at the North Pole. Suddenly, a man's voice

The pause that refreshes.

broke into her reverie. "Excuse me, ma'am. Are you going to be much longer?"

She turned around and there was a line of people with their shopping carts waiting to get into the freezer section. Flustered, she announced, "They seem to be out of fudge ripple ice cream."

A Senior Moment

Yet another cop story. The scene was Beverly Hills and I was on my way to pick up my daughter at school. I was coming up to a stop sign. I looked right. All clear. I looked left and noticed a police car. I kept right on going.

Sirens behind me. The cop pulled me over.

I was mortified. "Officer," I said, "I don't know why I did that. I saw the stop sign."

He was shaking his head in disbelief. "Miss," he said, "I must tell you, that was an existential experience for me."

"What do you mean?" I asked.

He said, "I looked at you. I saw you look at me. Then I saw you go through the stop sign, and I said to myself, 'Am I here? Do I exist?'"

What could I say. "Officer, I deserve the ticket."

"Yes, you do, but in what reality? On what plane of existence do I write it?"

He let me go without a ticket.

Never Old

I used to keep track of how many years I had left to live. When I turned thirty, I figured I had about forty, forty-five years to go. When I turned forty, I thought, I've lived half my life. When I hit fifty, I started thinking maybe I had thirty good years left in me. Now I laugh at myself. What a stupid exercise. The idea of diminished possible time is an illusion. Whether you're seven or seventy, you really just have the one moment you're living in now.

My mother, God love her, used to say, "I wouldn't be thirty again for all the tea in China. Look what I'm *not* missing." And she meant it. She also gave me a wonderful mind game one can play to soothe the passing of the decades. She once said that forty is younger than thirty-nine because forty is a beginning and thirty-nine is an end. I used it recently, telling myself I was *starting* my sixties, not wrapping up my fifties.

It's all in your state of mind. You can be happy growing older or you can be miserable, and it's in your power to make that choice for yourself.

When we were doing *The Mary Tyler Moore Show,* there was an episode that called for a woman in her seventies who was doddering and frail. The producer cast an actress who had been around Hollywood for decades. She was seventy-five. Despite her considerable experience, she just couldn't get the character right.

During a coffee break I asked the actress if she'd like help working on her lines and she agreed. She still couldn't get it right, and she was growing frustrated. "I should be able to do this," she said. "After all, *I'm* seventy-five myself." Suddenly, I realized. Of course. She was supposed to be playing a doddering old lady of seventy-five, but she didn't feel that way. She felt vital and healthy. The part didn't ring true for her. "Listen," I suggested, "try playing it like you're one hundred, not seventy-five." Presto! She became a little old lady. State of mind.

In 1900 the average life expectancy for a woman was fifty-five, so menopause did signal the end of life. Today, the average age of menopause is fifty-two, and the average life expectancy for a woman is eighty. The big question is, what are you going to do with the next thirty years of your life?

CHAPTER 6

TULKA

LIFTOFF!

Face It

Millie, a friend of many years, told me about a beauty trick used by legendary silent

Looking young is a full-time job.

screen star Dolores del Rio. Her advice was simple: Never open your mouth wide when you're laughing. To show mirth, part your lips slightly, toss your head back in a posture of great gaiety, and let the laughter drift from your throat. Make no lateral movement with your mouth that might result in laugh lines.

What women won't do to look young! I practiced the technique a few times with Millie, but it cracked us up so much that our lines were multiplying like crazy. Sorry, Dolores!

Being Fabulous

I get suspicious when I hear that phrase "fabulous at fifty." What does it mean? Don't we all get it by now that it means *looking* fabulous? That if you don't *look* fabulous, you can't *be* fabulous?

How about being fabulous as human

beings? Having fabulous awareness, manners, generosity? How about having a fabulous sense of humor, a capacity to love and laugh, interest in others? How about being fabulous to be around, being fabulous at listening, sharing, contributing, teaching, enjoying? How about being fabulous from within?

I know many women who are truly fabulous. It doesn't matter that they have lines on their faces, gray hair, extra pounds, extra veins, or extra chins.

And P.S.—the next time you are tempted to feel inadequate or envious when you see a dazzling fifty-plus woman beaming from a magazine cover, keep in mind that you are seeing the result of a day's work by a crew of professionals. Perfect lighting, a wind machine, special lenses and gels, and the all-important hair and makeup crew. We could all look spectacular if we had technicians following us around to cast the right glow. In fact, according to Webster's Collegiate Dictionary, the very word *fabulous* means "resembling a fable."

Would you rather be the stuff of fable, or a real woman? Both? I know, I know.

But the trivial pursuit of fabulousness crowds out so much life that could be lived and savored.

GENDER INEQUITY

A man with gray in his hair is considered "distinguished."

A woman with gray in her hair is "letting herself go." Why not call her hair ensilvered . . . moondusted?

A man with a weathered, lived-in face is described as rugged, with craggy good looks.

A woman needs only a few lines to be deemed haggard. Why not call her face eloquent?

A man of a certain age walks into a room and people take notice. He has gravitas.

A woman of a certain age walks into a room and she is invisible. Why is it so hard to see her allure?

Tough Toenails

How do you know you've reached that "certain age"? There are unmistakable, visible signs. For example . . .

- The hair on your head thins, but hair starts to appear in brand-new sites. You catch a side view in the mirror and see a single black hair hanging six inches from your chin.
- The veins in your legs start resembling a road map.
- You need your glasses to shave in the shower . . . until they fog up.
- Your upper arms start flapping in the wind . . . and even without wind.
- Your feet suddenly resemble something scary—vaguely reminiscent of those of a prehistoric lizard. Your toenails are so tough they shred the sheets.

Head south and take a right at the ankle.

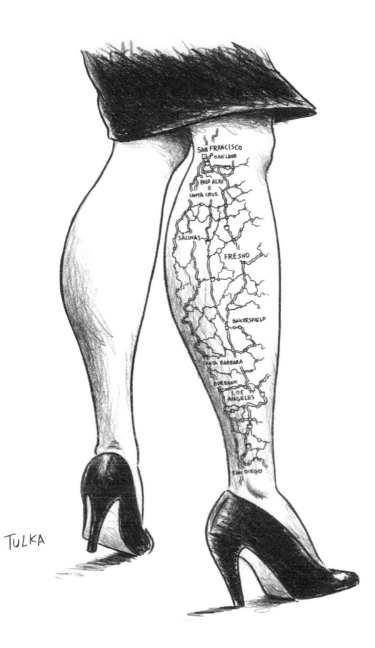

TULKA

Hard as nails.

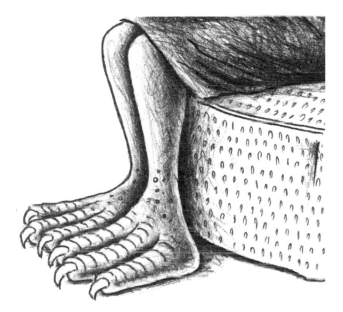

My Beautiful Draperies

Phyllis Diller, the perfectly marvelous comedienne, refers quite proudly to her upper arm droop as "my draperies." She says, "They're mine. They're beautiful. I've got something to show for all the years."

Phyllis made this remark to our mutual pal Joanne who was sweating herself into a puddle wearing turtlenecks and long sleeves during the sweltering Southern California summers. It completely changed Joanne's relationship to her arm jiggle. The other day she dropped by, arms laden with roses from her garden. She looked adorable in a bright turquoise, scoop-necked, sleeveless top—a cool, comfortable, great-looking sixty-nine-year-old.

"Thanks to Phyllis, I'm released from the tyranny of the coverup," she beamed.

Need a Lift?

"An instant face-lift is a smile," says Joanne. She's right, but some feel they need more help. I don't have anything against cosmetic surgery. I think it's just fine to give yourself a psychological lift with a youthful touchup. But in Hollywood there is such a desperation about looking young that women aren't just hiring surgeons, they're retaining contractors. Don't we all agree that certain people have gone off the deep end into the plastic surgery transformation pool and don't even remotely resemble themselves anymore? The transformation isn't from *old* to *young*. It's from *mature* to *scary*.

Blank lidless eyes that look like lizards in the Sahara sun. Puffy lips and grimacing smiles. I don't get it. I thought the purpose of plastic surgery was to look like a better rested, more youthful *you*.

If being young is the highest value, how can anyone be happy? If you live by the absurd notion that you must look like a

Don't droop when you can fly.

young girl, you may as well be living a scene from *The Fugitive*—always looking over your shoulder as time inexorably overtakes you.

So, if you're hitting the beautification— i.e., reconstruction—trail, here are a few questions to keep in mind:

- Will I be able to smile without looking as if I'm about to take a bite out of the person I'm talking to?
- Will my family recognize me? My dog?
- Will I be a candidate for a display at a mortician's convention?
- Will I look as if I'm standing in a 100-mph wind?
- Will I look as if I'm experiencing "lift-off"?
- Will I be able to muster more than one facial expression?

Another thing I don't quite get is the new trend involving shooting a quart of collagen into a woman's lips. In my experience, there are three ways to get lips like that—be a battered woman, get stung by a bee, or wear the big red wax kind that are popular at Halloween. A little enhancement is one thing. But you know you've gone too far when . . .

- Your lips obstruct your nasal passages.
- Kissing leaves bruises on your loved ones' faces.
- You have to spend a fortune on lipstick.
- You look like a guppy. Or a puffer fish. Or a grouper.
- Your lips enter a room five minutes before you do.
- Your lips are bigger than your head.

I have a beautiful, amazing neighbor and friend named Feliza. She was a Vanderbilt for a time in her youth. Now eighty, Feliza is a powerhouse. She walks a mile every day, gardens, bakes, and generally never sits still. Over lunch one day I asked, "Did you ever think about having plastic surgery?"

Before . . . and *Aaaaarghhh!!!*

"Betty, is that you?"

"Oh, I don't have the time, Val," she replied, "and if I did, I wouldn't."

"Wouldn't have the surgery?"

"No, the time," she said with a twinkle. "I don't have the time to think about having the surgery."

It's not even on her radar screen. As Feliza is living it, eighty looks great!

Badges of Honor

Will we reach the point when the new sign of old age will be the overcorrected face? "Wow! Look at all the work she's had done. She must be one hundred and three!"

Wrinkles should be a sign of having lived, having put in some time and put out a ton of energy. Creases, lines, age spots, sags should be badges of honor for having stayed in the game of life and participating full-out.

We need to appreciate the time put in on the planet by the owner of a face with such obviously earned credits.

The new face of old age could be the real one, not a plastic mock-up. A face full of experience, knowledge, humor, and peace.

Each of my lines is a badge of honor.

Key:

a. *Son hits ball through neighbor's window.*

b. *Husband forgets anniversary.*

c. *Dog has puppies.*

d. *Basement floods.*

e. *Make 5,000 cookies for school bake sale.*

f. *Credit card canceled.*

g. *Win tennis tournament.*

h. *Teenager totals car.*

i. *Debt from daughter's wedding.*

j. *Husband retires.*

k. *Daughter divorces.*

l. *A lifetime of laughter.*

TULKA

CHAPTER 7

HUMOR REPLACEMENT THERAPY

———

Let's Vent

I think midlife women crave humor. They crave honesty and understanding. When I get together with my women friends, we end up on the floor laughing—at our lives, our men, our hangups, our appetites, and our fantasies. I'm glad that we've overcome that need we had when we were younger to pretend everything was fine when it wasn't. Today we *vent* with abandon! I come away from these sessions with a lighter heart, a more ironic view of my world. It energizes me.

While you're scouring the shelves of your local health food store for the latest in yam creams, metabolic coolants, mood stabilizers, and other remedies on the menopausal "must have" list, don't forget to pick up a gallon of laughs. Without humor, midlife can be as dry as your—well, let's just say it can be a drag.

Did you know there is scientific research that actually equates good health with humor? Humor has been shown to reduce stress, raise your pain threshold, and boost your immune system. In one study, people listening to twenty minutes of Lily Tomlin doing her telephone operator routine were much less sensitive to pain than those listening to an academic lecture.

Have More Fun in Bed

An elegant matron swept up to me on a wave of perfume one day while I was walking my dog, Archie. I was dressed in old sweats and a slouchy hat, and she looked as if she'd just stepped out of a Christian Dior showroom. "My dear!" she cried. "I must tell you. You have given me more pleasure in bed than *any* of my husbands." That was high praise indeed. I realized that she was referring to the reruns of *The Mary Tyler Moore Show* and *Rhoda* that air between midnight and two A.M.

The Girlfriend Factor

Erma Bombeck wrote, "A friend will tell you the truth about your culottes." A friend never defends a husband who gets his wife an electric skillet for her birthday. A

Now that's *entertainment!*

TULKA

friend will tell you she saw your old boyfriend—and he's a priest."

I'm blessed with a group of girlfriends who are frank, funny, upbeat, and not afraid to call a liver spot a liver spot. We love each other dearly. Since we're all taking the same ride—we try to make the most of it.

To me, one of the best things about *The Mary Tyler Moore Show* was that it gave great girlfriend. Mary and Rhoda were opposites in many ways, but they kept their criticisms of each other within the space of love and friendship.

Rhoda would see Mary wimping out and say, "Mary, please, when are you gonna stand up for yourself? Don't take that from him." Mary would see Rhoda making crazy choices, and she'd say, "Rhoda, why are you dating that guy? He spends your money, he sees other women, he spends your money *on* other women. Do you really think so little of yourself?" One of my favorite lines was "You, Mary, will marry a crowned head of Europe. I, on the other hand, will eat three

hundred peanut butter cups and die."
Girlfriends.

The irony is that Mary and Rhoda were originally conceived as adversaries, but the writers had the relationship quickly evolve. With Phyllis, played by Cloris Leachman, we became a triangle. Rhoda and Phyllis sniping, with Mary in the middle, but girlfriends in spite of it. What fun we had!

Over the Top

My friend Arlene used to organize afternoon tea parties for her women friends at a place called Trumps in Beverly Hills. During one of these teas, someone suggested that at a certain age, a woman should avoid being on top during lovemaking. "Gravity does terrible things to your face," she said sagely. Just what I wanted to hear over Darjeeling and scones! Later, by telephone, Arlene and I each put a makeup mirror on our respective tables and leaned our faces over to have a look. We shrieked with horror and hilarity as we watched sags form. Our tea party pal had a point. Try it for yourself, but don't freak out. There are choices:

1. Stay off the top.
2. Be on top and dim the lights.
3. Be on top and to hell with your sagging face.

A friend shared these insights with me:

The older a woman gets, the stronger her libido gets.

The older a man gets, the weaker his libido gets.

An older woman will never wake you up in the middle of the night to ask, "What are you thinking?" An older woman doesn't care what you think.

Meno Funnies

Thank God for humor! And thank God for women who have introduced a whole new world of funnies specifically designed for midlife women. Let me mention my two favorites:

MINNIE PAUZ

On the Internet: www.minniepauz.com
Phone: 248-969-3937

Minnie Pauz is a cartoon character created by midlife cartoonist Dee Adams. Minnie's "natural" prescription for menopause is humor. Click on to the website and laugh your socks off at over seventy cartoons. You'll learn something, too. There's solid information and sharing involved. You can also get T-shirts and coffee mugs featuring Minnie stating, "I'm just a Rebel with the Pause."

HEATWAVE

On the Internet: www.menomaven.com
Phone: 877-660-9771 (toll free)

Jackie Brookman, creator of Minerva the Menopausal Maven, came up with the idea of helping menopausal women take a progressive journey (guided by Minerva) from Hormone Hell to Hormone Heights. The Heatwave Card Conversations is a card deck of sixty-six cards in six categories, each with its own dose of wit and wisdom. Here are some examples, compliments of Minerva:

Menomoment: I met someone I hadn't seen in fifteen years and she said, "You look great and healthy." I heard, "You look old and fat."

Minerva's Response: First things first. Get your hearing checked for compliment comprehension. Seems to be an audibility problem there.

Menomoment: I have very little interest in sex for the first time in my adult life. I'd rather go shopping.

Minerva's Response: Listless Low Libido: You are in luck. Your estrogen may be low, but your brain, the greatest erogenous zone in your body, is still working! On your next spree, acquire an aphrodisiac: a nasty, naughty novel for nightly noctural emissions. Whoa, is it getting hot in here or what??

Don't Cry for Me

Let me tell you a secret about being a sixty-plus woman. It's a blast. I'm more comfortable with *me* than I've ever been before. It's easier for me to say, "No." I seem to be laughing more and worrying less. Maybe I don't have the sexual appeal I had when I was thirty, and that's fine because I'm not interested in attracting men anyway. What's wonderful is that, finally, I feel relaxed in my own skin.

CHAPTER 8

IMAGINE THAT!

Wouldn't It Be Great?

I've heard it said that if you can imagine something, you can make it real. So, imagine this:

- Wouldn't it be great if we didn't care so much what other people thought of us?
- Wouldn't it be great if we could be outrageous and not be terrified of the consequences?
- Wouldn't it be great if looking good wasn't tied up with looking young?
- Wouldn't it be great if we were proud of our gray hairs?
- Wouldn't it be great if we could acknowledge how well we roll with the punches?
- Wouldn't it be great if we could really act our age?

Get Over It

What's holding you back from living fully? Is it fear? Let's look at this terrible, terrifying thing called aging. It breaks my heart when I hear a woman in her thirties say, "I'm getting old." In that state of mind she's got no chance of experiencing fully her thirties. Susan, a comedy writer friend of mine, related what her mom recently confessed: "When I became fifty I realized that I was old. Now I'm sixty and I wish I could be as young as fifty!" This is the human pattern of longing that gets in the way of living.

We fear aging for a lot of reasons. The expectation of failing health, the loss of status, the prospect of being alone, and the uncertainty—"What is going to become of me?" A person can be frozen with fear if she spends too much time imagining that the Grim Reaper is sharpening his blade. I think the best way to beat back the fear of death is to *live*—actively choose to live as full-out as you can.

What's holding you back from loving fully? Is it anger? Those old grievances, jealousies, and arguments drag you down and age you more than anything else. Two very dear friends of mine had a major falling out over a minor thing some fifteen years ago.

"Come on, girls. Lift those minds!"

They stopped speaking. Recently, I arranged a luncheon and invited them both, without telling either who was coming. What I'd hoped for happened. In an instant, with tears and hugs, the bitter feelings were erased. Life really *is* too short.

Mental Aerobics

My kid sister, Ginger, successful attorney and mom, once said, "People spend so much time, money, and effort on physical fitness. How about a little *mental* fitness. Read a book!"

I wish there were aerobics studios that specialized in mental fitness. The instructor would be licensed by Mensa. She'd line us up and shout, "Come on, girls, work those brain muscles!"

With Mozart booming on the stereo, we'd chant, "E equals mc squared. DNA stands for deoxyribonucleic acid and is the blueprint of the human cell."

The electricity emanating from our heads would be—well, *heady.*

"Come on, break a sweat! What's the capital of Bangladesh? Spell proletariat— P-R-O-L-E-T-A-R-I-A-T. Name the great women of the twentieth century—Margaret Sanger . . . Golda Meir . . . Toni Morrison . . . Hillary Clinton . . . work those muscles!"

Valerie's Golden Rules

Now that I've passed age sixty, these rules are more important to me than ever.

1. Set your own terms.

Decide what really matters to you. Don't chase after false glories or live by others' rules. I learned my lesson the day I found out that someone was marketing Valerie

"You'll make a great refrigerator magnet someday."

Harper refrigerator magnets. Can you imagine chasing after fame so you can be immortalized on a magnet stuck to a refrigerator?

2. Overdo it.

When I was young, I had boundless energy and a tendency to overdo. My mother was always telling me, "Valerie, don't overdo it." As I matured, I realized that, given the state of the world, maybe others were *under*-doing it.

3. Give it a new spin.

Question what you've automatically accepted as so. For example: Cellulite is biologically positive. Why not decide to *adore* cellulite?

4. Get interested.

Stop working so hard at being *interesting* and focus on what's outside yourself. There are universes out there that need to be explored. And, an *interested* person is extremely *interesting*.

5. Relax.

Realize that it's all going to turn out. You don't have to be a feverish ball of nervous tension. Put an end to white-knuckle living and create your own inner peace and quiet.

6. Trust yourself.

Self-doubt is immobilizing. Given the years you've lived, you deserve to have some confidence. Way back, my big sister, Leah, gave me some great advice: "Laugh when you can, cry if you must, but keep moving."

7. Be the one.

A friend told me that what bothers her about being older is having people assume that it's all over for her, even though she feels so vital, alert, and *young*. Well, you can't change the culture overnight. But you can change yourself. Change starts with you.

WOACAs Unite!

We are Women of a Certain Age—WOACA. It's pronounced WOE-ah-ka, but don't start saying, "Woe is me." To the contrary.

As a WOACA you are released from a certain prison. You suffer less curtailment of movement. Strange and creepy guys no longer whistle and make lewd comments when you walk down the street. You can come and go as you please with dignity.

When you were younger, perhaps you found that your identity was completely wrapped up in whether or not a man was interested in you. I know that was true for me. You are freed from that prison, too. No longer do you have to wait for the phone to ring, or to be asked to dance, or to be kissed awake by Prince Charming.

Women are served by the power shift that occurs as we age. Run with your freedom and don't fret that you're not what you used to be. You are what you are now—and you couldn't be this "you" without the years. So take heart. Live it up and walk tall. You're a ma'am!

As that great role model of WOACA, Sophia Loren, once said, "There is a fountain of youth. It is your mind, your talents, the creativity you bring to your life and the lives of the people you love. When you learn to tap this source, you will truly have defeated age."

Let's give ourselves a hand.